Causes of the American Revolution

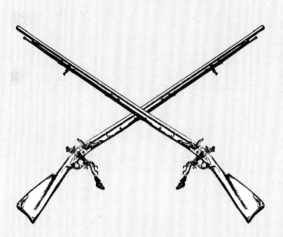

ROAD TO WAR
CAUSES OF CONFLICT

Causes of the American Revolution

Richard M. Strum

OTTN
PUBLISHING
STOCKTON, NJ

DEDICATION

In memory of my father, Norman Eugene Strum (1936–1999).

OTTN Publishing
16 Risler Street
Stockton, NJ 08859
www.ottnpublishing.com

3 5 7 9 8 6 4

Library of Congress Cataloging-in-Publication Data

   Strum, Richard M.
    Causes of the American Revolution / Richard M. Strum.
      p. cm. — (Road to war)
    Summary: "Discusses and explains the events of the 1750s, 1760s, and 1770s that contributed to the start of the American Revolution"—Provided by publisher.
    Includes bibliographical references and index.
    ISBN-13: 978-1-59556-001-8
    ISBN-10: 1-59556-001-7
    ISBN-13: 978-1-59556-005-6 (pbk.)
    ISBN-10: 1-59556-005-X (pbk.)
    1. United States—History—Revolution, 1775-1783—Causes—Juvenile literature. 2. United States—Politics and government—To 1775—Juvenile literature. 3. Great Britain—Politics and government—1760-1789—Juvenile literature. 4. World politics—18th century. I. Title. II. Series.
    E210.S88 2006
    973.3'11—dc22

                                   2005006797

Frontispiece: British troops fire on a mob in Boston, an incident that would become known as the "Boston Massacre," March 5, 1770.

Table of Contents

Notable Figures

ADAMS, JOHN (1735–1826). A Massachusetts delegate to the Continental Congress, Adams was appointed in 1776 to the committee responsible for drafting the Declaration of Independence; later he served as one of the three American commissioners who negotiated the peace treaty officially ending the Revolutionary War; he served as George Washington's vice president and, in 1796, was elected the second president of the United States.

ADAMS, SAMUEL (1722–1803). A leader of the Sons of Liberty in Boston, Adams was a vocal critic of the Sugar Act and the Stamp Act; he was a member of the Massachusetts delegation to the First and Second Continental Congress, where he was an early champion of independence; he later served as governor of Massachusetts.

DICKINSON, JOHN (1732–1808). A lawyer by training, Dickinson encouraged colonial opposition to the Stamp Act and other British policies, but he consistently argued for a peaceful resolution of the colonies' grievances; as a member of the Pennsylvania delegation to the Second Continental Congress, he refused to sign the Declaration of Independence.

FRANKLIN, BENJAMIN (1706–1790). A man of wide-ranging accomplishments, Franklin represented Pennsylvania at the Albany Congress in 1754, at the Second Continental Congress in 1776, and at the Constitutional Convention in 1787; he was a member of the committee that drafted the Declaration of Independence and served on the three-man commission that negotiated the peace treaty with Great Britain.

John Adams   Sam Adams   Ben Franklin

GAGE, THOMAS (1721–1787). The commander of British forces in North America, General Gage was appointed governor of Massachusetts in 1774; his decision to seize colonists' stores of gunpowder and firearms sparked the Battle of Lexington and Concord, the first engagement of the Revolutionary War.

GEORGE III (1738–1820). King of Great Britain and Ireland from 1760 until his death, he alienated many American colonists with his heavy-handed policies.

HANCOCK, JOHN (1737–1793). As president of the Provisional Congress of Massachusetts, Hancock—a wealthy Boston merchant—ordered militia units, known as "minutemen," to be formed in 1774 and 1775; he also served as president of the Continental Congress from 1775 to 1777, as president of the United States under the Articles of Confederation (1785–1786), and as a nine-term governor of Massachusetts.

HENRY, PATRICK (1736–1799). In May 1765, while serving in his first year as a member of Virginia's legislature (the House of Burgesses), Henry proposed the Virginia Stamp Act Resolutions, which contended that the king and Parliament could not tax the colonists; his most famous speech ("give me liberty or give me death!") occurred in March 1775, when he asked the legislature for troops to defend Virginia from the British.

HUTCHINSON, THOMAS (1711–1780). As royal governor of Massachusetts, the Boston-born Hutchinson

King George III

John Hancock

Patrick Henry

steadfastly upheld British authority; his refusal to permit ships to leave Boston Harbor until their cargoes of tea had been unloaded helped lead to the Boston Tea Party in December 1773.

JEFFERSON, THOMAS (1743–1826). Credited with writing the Declaration of Independence in 1776, Jefferson later served as U.S. secretary of state and vice president before winning election as the third president of the United States.

PAINE, THOMAS (1737–1809). A political philosopher, he published a highly influential pamphlet, *Common Sense*, in January 1776; it urged the colonies to declare their independence from England.

RANDOLPH, PEYTON (CA. 1721–1775). Speaker of the Virginia House of Burgesses, he was elected president of the First and Second Continental Congress; he championed the Patriot cause but died about eight months before the Declaration of Independence.

REVERE, PAUL (1735–1818). A silversmith and engraver, he is best known for his famous night ride of April 18, 1775, during which he warned Massachusetts Patriots of the British advance on Lexington and Concord.

SEARS, ISAAC (1730–1786). A longtime leader of the Sons of Liberty in New York, Sears organized protests against the Stamp Act and later marshaled mobs to seize the New York arsenal and the customs house following the Battle of Lexington and Concord.

Thomas Jefferson   Thomas Paine   Peyton Randolph

TOWNSHEND, CHARLES (1725–1767). As Britain's Chancellor of the Exchequer (chief finance minister), he favored making the American colonies pay import duties on products such as lead, paint, paper, glass, and tea; the Townshend Acts greatly angered the American colonists and helped lead to the Revolutionary War.

WASHINGTON, GEORGE (1732–1799). A Virginia delegate to the First and Second Continental Congress, Washington was selected to be commander-in-chief of the Continental Army in June 1775; six years later, with French assistance, he forced the British surrender at Yorktown, Virginia; in 1787 he presided over the Constitutional Convention, and in 1789 he took office as the first president of the United States.

April 19, 1775

British troops fire into a line of minutemen on Lexington Green, killing eight Americans. Dr. Joseph Warren (bottom left), a leader of the Boston Patriots, had ordered the minutemen to be warned that the British were on the march. Battles at Lexington and Concord on April 19, 1775, marked the start of the American Revolution.

So it had come to this! His Majesty's troops had marched out of Boston in the early hours of April 19, 1775. They were coming to Lexington. The Lexington *militia* formed on the green, waiting. Known as *minutemen* because they could be ready at a minute's notice, the men had awakened as riders passed through town with a message from Boston: "The Regulars are Coming!"

Step by step, Great Britain and her American colonies had grown apart. Just 15 years earlier, British regular soldiers and *provincial* militiamen fought side by side against a common enemy—the French empire. For seven years war raged on the frontiers of Britain's North American colonies. With the fall of Montreal in 1760, the war came to an end, and with it the French empire in North America.

However, the same war that brought British and provincial troops together also sowed the seeds of discontent. The war against France proved costly, and the British government needed new sources of revenue. Members of *Parliament* and His Majesty King George III viewed the American colonies as a potential source of new income.

New taxes imposed on the American colonies, such as the Stamp Act of 1765 and taxes on tea and other British goods, drove a wedge between the mother country and the colonists. But the actions of the British Parliament also created disagreements among the colonists themselves. Not everyone in the 13 American colonies saw eye to eye on the issues of the day. Some colonists supported the right of the king and Parliament to raise taxes in the colonies. Others believed that such taxation was wrong, but even those colonists could not agree on the correct way to resist. A few radical leaders, like Isaac Sears in New York and Samuel Adams in Boston, believed that throwing off British rule was the only way to guarantee the colonists' freedoms. Others, including Pennsylvania's Benjamin Franklin and Virginia's George Washington, supported many *petitions* that implored the king to change his policies.

By 1774, the British government was fed up with the colonists' resistance to taxation. In response to the Boston Tea Party—a protest against the tax on tea in December 1773—the British prime minister, Lord North, ordered the port of Boston to be closed to trading ships until the colonists paid for the destroyed tea.

In September 1774, representatives from 12 of the colonies met in Philadelphia, the largest city in the colonies, to discuss their *grievances* against Great Britain and to send their demands to the king. Among the men in attendance at the First Continental Congress were George Washington, Samuel Adams, and John Adams. Upon adjourning, the delegates agreed to convene the Second Continental Congress in May 1775.

Meanwhile, the king's troops continued to create hardships for the colonists. In Williamsburg, Virginia, the royal governor, Lord Dunmore, ordered British marines from a Royal Navy vessel in the York River to

Paul Revere, William Dawes, and Samuel Prescott rode through the countryside around Boston to warn the minutemen that the British Army was on the march.

seize the store of black powder from the public *magazine*—powder belonging to the Virginia militia, not the British troops. Tempers flared, but violence was averted—at least for the time being.

As the spring of 1775 approached, tensions in Boston grew. General Thomas Gage, the commander of all British forces in North America, ordered troops out into the countryside around Boston to *confiscate* powder and weapons. General Gage believed the colonists had a large store of these in Concord. Before dawn on April 19, 1775, about 700 British regular soldiers marched for Concord. Their move was expected.

Most colonists still considered themselves British citizens, so as Paul Revere and others rode through the countryside, they did not shout, "The British are Coming!" After all, they were British too. Revere and the others shouted, "The Regulars are Coming! The Regulars are Coming!"—meaning the British troops.

By dawn, about 80 men, many carrying their muskets, waited restlessly on the Lexington Green. Most no doubt hoped that a show of force might persuade the British to turn around and return to Boston. As the sun rose, the British troops came into view—the soldiers in their brick-red uniforms, the officers wearing bright scarlet coats that glistened in the sunlight.

The British officers yelled at the minutemen to disperse—to leave the green and go home. At first no one moved. Then the minutemen began to disband slowly. Suddenly, a shot rang out. To this day, no one knows who fired first, but soon British troops and minutemen were exchanging fire. After a few volleys, the British officers shouted orders, whereupon their men re-formed into columns and continued toward Concord.

On Lexington Green, eight minutemen lay dead. The American War of Independence had begun.

Britain's American Colonies

The Pilgrims pray on board ship during an early stage of their voyage to North America. In 1620, the Pilgrims founded Plymouth Colony in present-day Massachusetts. Other British colonies would follow. When William Penn (bottom left) founded Pennsylvania in 1681, he promised religious freedom and permitted democratic elections of government officials.

With the arrival of Christopher Columbus in the New World in 1492, an era of European exploration and *colonization* in the Western Hemisphere began. Over the next 200 years, European countries established colonies throughout North and South America. In South America, Spain and Portugal dominated. In North America, Spain was joined by Great Britain, France, Holland, and Sweden.

After a failed attempt to establish a colony on Roanoke Island in 1587, the British established their first permanent settlement in North America at Jamestown in 1607. Within a decade, British settlements in the colony of Virginia stretched along the coast of the Chesapeake Bay.

The main reason for the Virginia settlements was to make money. In the 16th century, huge amounts of gold and silver had flowed into the Spanish treasury from South America and Mexico, making Spain one of the richest and most powerful countries in the world

Colonists construct the Jamestown settlement during the spring of 1607. This colony in Virginia became the first permanent English settlement in North America.

Barrels of valuable tobacco are loaded onto a ship in Virginia for transport to Britain.

(and enriching many Spanish conquerors and colonists as well). The British monarchs Queen Elizabeth I, and later King James I, wanted a share of the New World's rich resources—which would help their nation rival Spain's power. And the key to exploiting the resources of the New World was to establish colonies there.

The British colonists did not find gold in Virginia, but they soon found something nearly as valuable— tobacco. The Native Americans of *tidewater* Virginia introduced the British settlers in Jamestown to the plant, and soon smoking tobacco had become a fashionable *craze*, both in Virginia and in Europe. The *fast fact...*

While the founders of the Plymouth and Massachusetts Bay colonies sought religious freedom for themselves, they did not welcome settlers who worshipped differently. Rhode Island and Maryland, on the other hand, welcomed all settlers regardless of their religious beliefs.

colonists in Virginia grew tobacco as a *cash crop*, shipping it back to Britain in exchange for money or goods needed in the colony.

In 1620, a new group of settlers embarked for the New World. These colonists were not seeking wealth. Rather, they hoped to find a place where they could practice their religion freely. Called *Nonconformists* because they refused to follow the ways of the Church of England, or Anglican Church, these settlers were better known as the Pilgrims. The Pilgrims landed in Massachusetts and began the Plymouth Colony. Other Nonconformists seeking religious freedom soon followed. The Puritans—so called because they sought to purify the Anglican Church by simplifying its ceremonies—settled Massachusetts Bay Colony to the north of Plymouth. By the end of the 1600s, Massachusetts Bay had absorbed Plymouth Colony.

Other European nations also started colonies on the Atlantic coast of North America. The French established Quebec in 1608. In the 1620s, the Dutch established New Netherlands and its capital city of New Amsterdam at the mouth of the Hudson River. Sweden established New Sweden at the mouth of the Delaware River in the 1630s.

Besides Massachusetts Bay and Virginia, other British colonies grew along the coast of New England and in Pennsylvania, Maryland, and the Carolinas. Over time, the British also gained control of the Dutch and Swedish colonies, which became New York, New Jersey, and Delaware.

Of course, the land claimed by the colonists was not uninhabited when they arrived. Numerous Native American tribes populated the Atlantic coast of North America before European contact. Between 1607 and 1754, however, diseases carried by the Europeans, in addition to armed conflicts with the settlers, decimated the Indian population. Survivors moved west and north.

One of the strongest groups of Native Americans in the middle of the 18th century was the Iroquois Nations, a confederacy comprising the Onondaga, Oneida, Seneca, Cayuga, Mohawk, and Tuscarora peoples. As tensions between the French and British rose, representatives from seven of the British colonies invited the leaders of the Iroquois to Albany, New York, in 1754. The Albany Congress sought reassurances that if war broke out between Britain and France, the Iroquois would side with the British, as they had in past conflicts.

However, the colonial representatives also discussed a plan for a defensive union of the colonies. Benjamin Franklin, from Pennsylvania, proposed the

Colonial representatives meet outside a hall in Albany, 1754. At the Albany Congress, a plan to unite the colonies was proposed, but it was never approved or implemented.

This famous illustration representing the need for colonial unity appeared in Ben Franklin's *Pennsylvania Gazette*, May 9, 1754.

creation of a "Grand Council" to oversee the defense of the colonies, regulate westward expansion, and negotiate with the Indians. While the colonial legislatures would elect representatives to the Grand Council, the king would appoint its president. After the Albany Congress, the various colonial representatives took Franklin's proposal back to their legislatures. Although the legislatures ultimately failed to take action on setting up the Grand Council, the idea of 13 separate colonies working together would rise again.

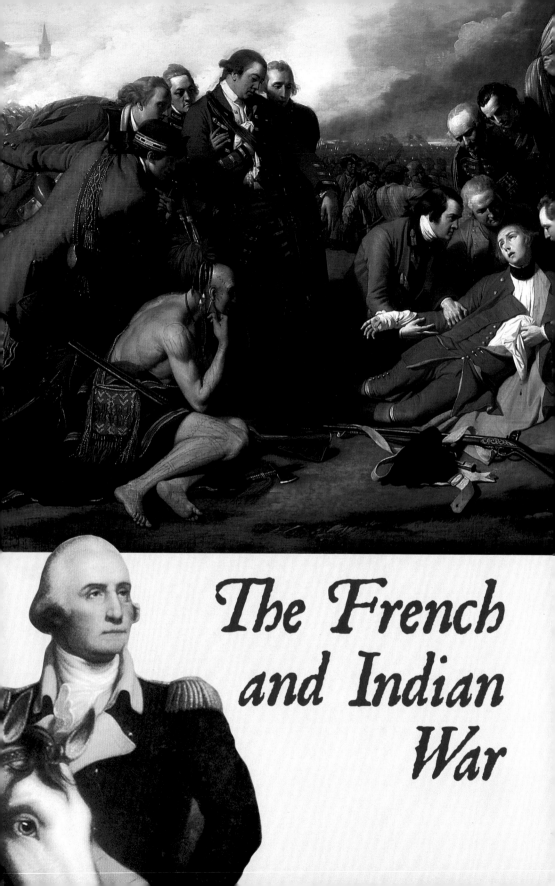

The French and Indian War

British officers surround their leader, General James Wolfe, who was mortally wounded during an attack on the French city of Quebec, September 1759. The French and Indian War ended in victory for the British. During this conflict, George Washington (bottom left) and other colonials gained their first military experience.

By the late 1600s, the boundaries of the French and British colonies met along the northern and western borders of New England, New York, Pennsylvania, and Virginia. Beginning in 1689, French and British colonists fought each other in a series of conflicts that formed part of larger wars originating in Europe and pitting France against Great Britain. Among the British colonists in North America, each was named for the ruler of Great

Britain at the time of the war. The War of the League of Augsburg (1689–1697) in Europe was known as King William's War in North America. Likewise, colonists in North America called the War of the Spanish Succession (1702–1713) Queen Anne's War. From 1740 to 1748, the War of the Austrian Succession raged in Europe; it was known as King George's War in the American colonies.

The Treaty of Aix-la-Chapelle, which ended King George's War, established the border between the French and British colonies in North America. However, neither France nor Great Britain was satisfied. A key region claimed by both countries was the Ohio River valley.

The French sought control of the Ohio Country (as the territory west of the Appalachian Mountains and north of the Ohio River was called) primarily for its rich supply of furs and as a connection between Canada and the French territories of Illinois and Louisiana. Together, these three territories made up New France. The economy of New France was built on trading goods to the Native Americans of the region in exchange for animal furs, which were highly valued in Europe. Beyond the St. Lawrence Valley in Quebec, France's territory was sparsely settled.

On the other hand, the British colonies wanted to

expand into the Ohio River valley and occupy the land. Most British colonists made a living by farming. As more and more British immigrants arrived in the American colonies, farmland along the Atlantic coast became scarce. By expanding west, colonies like Pennsylvania and Virginia hoped to find more farmland.

To support their claim to the Ohio River valley, the French built a series of forts from Lake Erie to the forks of the Ohio River (the site of present-day Pittsburgh, Pennsylvania). Concerned that the French were building forts in territory claimed by his colony, Robert Dinwiddie, Virginia's lieutenant governor, sent a young officer in the Virginia militia to the Ohio Country with a message demanding that the French leave. George Washington was 21 years old when he journeyed through the wilderness to deliver his message. While the French treated him with respect, they refused to accept Governor Dinwiddie's message. The French commander at Fort LeBoeuf told Washington that only Governor Duquesne in Quebec City could reply to the Virginia governor's demands.

Unhappy with the French response, Virginia sent George Washington back to the Ohio Country in the spring of 1754, with orders to build a fort at the forks of the Ohio. He arrived only to discover the French already hard at work constructing Fort Duquesne.

Following a skirmish between Washington's troops and a French force, in which a French diplomat was killed, Washington soon found himself surrounded at the hastily built Fort Necessity. Washington was forced to surrender, but the French allowed him and his men to return to Virginia with the message that the Ohio River valley belonged to the king of France. Washington's defeat at Fort Necessity marked the start of the French and Indian War in North America. The conflict, which soon expanded into a world war, was known as the Seven Years' War in Europe.

In 1755, for the third year in a row, the valley of the Ohio took center stage in the conflict between the French and British in North America. General Edward Braddock led a force of British and provincial troops toward Fort Duquesne. On July 9, the French and their Indian allies ambushed Braddock's soldiers, delivering a crushing defeat. Wounded in the battle, Braddock soon died, and the British withdrew.

The fighting shifted to the northeast in September 1755, when a large British army moved to attack the French stronghold of Fort St. Frederic on Lake Champlain. A French and Canadian force met the army at the southern end of Lake George on September 8, 1755. While the British won the Battle of Lake George, the attack stopped them from moving further

Colonial militiamen return Indian fire in this somewhat inaccurate depiction of the July 1755 Battle of Monongahela. The British defeat opened frontier settlements in Virginia, Maryland, and Pennsylvania to Indian attacks.

north that fall. The British began constructing Fort William Henry at the southern end of Lake George; 35 miles north, the French built Fort Carillon at Ticonderoga.

In 1756 and 1757, the French, under the command of Louis-Joseph, marquis de Montcalm, met with success at Fort Oswego on Lake Ontario and at Fort William Henry. In 1758, the largest battle of the war in North America was fought at Fort Carillon. British general James Abercromby amassed a force of more than 16,000 British and provincial troops to attack the French at Ticonderoga. General

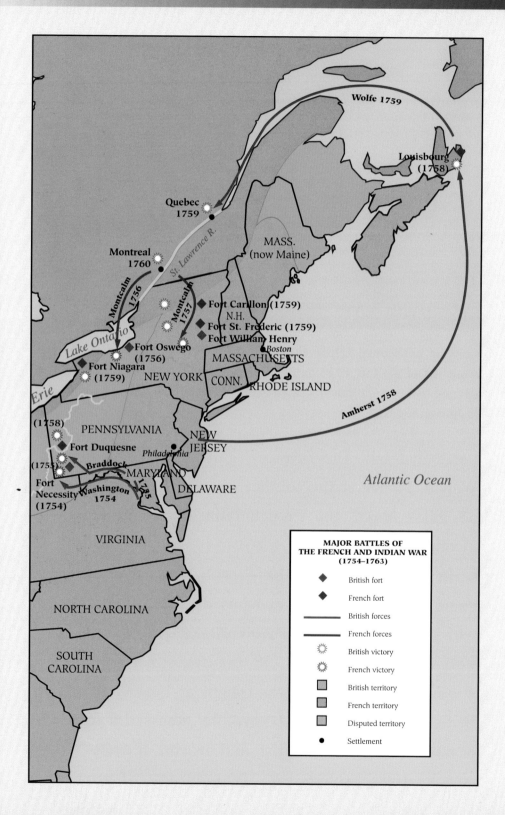

Wolfe 1759

Louisbourg
(1758)

Quebec
1759

St. Lawrence R.

Montreal
1760

MASS.
(now Maine)

Montcalm 1756

Montcalm
1757

Fort Carillon (1759)
N.H.
Fort St. Frederic (1759)
Fort William Henry
Boston

Fort Oswego
(1756)

Lake Ontario

MASSACHUSETTS

Fort Niagara
(1759)

NEW YORK   CONN.

RHODE ISLAND

Erie

Amherst 1758

(1758)

PENNSYLVANIA

Fort Duquesne   Philadelphia

NEW
JERSEY

Atlantic Ocean

(1755)   Braddock

Fort
Necessity Washington
(1754)   1754

MARYLAND

DELAWARE

1755

VIRGINIA

NORTH CAROLINA

SOUTH
CAROLINA

**MAJOR BATTLES OF
THE FRENCH AND INDIAN WAR
(1754–1763)**

◆   British fort

◆   French fort

——   British forces

——   French forces

✹   British victory

✹   French victory

▨   British territory

▨   French territory

▨   Disputed territory

●   Settlement

Montcalm, in command at Carillon, had only 3,500 soldiers available to defend Ticonderoga. But when the two sides met at the Battle of Carillon on July 8, 1758, the outnumbered French took advantage of *defensive works* to defeat the British.

The tide began to turn for the British later in 1758, however. In late July, forces under General Jeffery Amherst captured Fortress Louisbourg on Cape Breton Island. A British and provincial force under General John Forbes captured Fort Duquesne in November 1758.

By 1759, the British and their colonial troops were closing in on French Canada. The French abandoned Forts Carillon and St. Frederic on Lake Champlain, and Fort Niagara on Lake Ontario. And in September, they lost the Battle of the Plains of Abraham at Quebec City. The French surrender of Montreal in 1760 marked the end of French rule in Canada. The war officially concluded three years later.

But while the British had won the French and Indian War, victory had not come cheaply. And, as it turned out, British efforts to raise money to pay for the war would set in motion events that ultimately led to the loss of the very colonial territories Britain had fought France to secure.

Under the "Liberty Tree," Bostonians force a British tax agent who has been tarred and feathered to drink a pot of tea. This cartoon appeared in a colonial newspaper in 1774.

4

Parliament vs. Colonial Legislatures

F ighting the French in North America and across Europe had strained the British treasury. Members of Parliament protested against the heavy burden of taxation on the citizens of the British Isles. Why not, they wondered, have the American colonies help pay for the war? After all, they argued, had not the British Empire spent large amounts of money for armies and navies to protect the colonists from the French?

In addition to paying off the war debts, Parliament had to address the issue of how to administer the large new North American territories Great Britain had won from France. All of Canada and the Illinois Country came under British control in 1763 with the end of the Seven Years' War in Europe. These territories contained not only French settlers but also numerous Native Americans. The British had to find ways to rule their newly acquired territories without upsetting the residents.

In 1763, the Ottawa chief Pontiac led a rebellion of Indian peoples against British rule in former French territories along the western frontier. Many of the rebelling Indians had been Britain's allies during the war with France. Now, they feared an influx of colonists pushing westward into their territories. To keep peace with the Native Americans on the western frontier, the king issued a royal *proclamation* in 1763. This proclamation prohibited colonists from settling west of the Appalachian Mountains. At least on paper, this would prevent conflicts between Indians and colonists. In reality, the proclamation had little effect on settlement across the Atlantic Ocean.

One of the difficulties Great Britain faced after the French and Indian War was that the colonial legislatures had grown accustomed to running the colonies with little interference from Britain. While royal governors represented the king, they often allowed the legislatures great latitude in the business of day-to-day governance. Over the previous century, the colonists had gotten used to unofficial self-government.

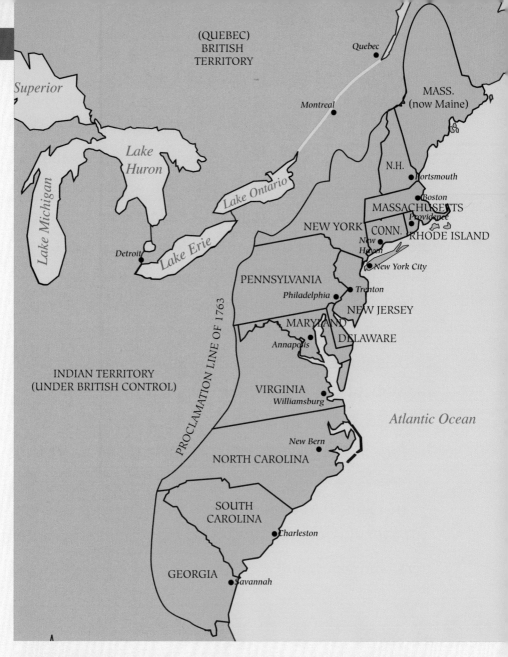

The Proclamation of 1763 established the western boundary of the British colonies. Many colonial leaders resented the king's effort to limit the expansion of American settlements.

Great Britain's plans to pay off its massive war debts included taxes on the American colonies. The Sugar Act of 1763 imposed taxes on sugar and other goods imported by the colonies. The tax on molasses, a key ingredient for making rum, was three pence per gallon. This was actually a tax cut—the tax on molasses since 1733 had been six pence per gallon— but in the past customs officials had seldom collected the money due. The Sugar Act included new enforcement methods to make sure colonists paid the taxes. These included trying smuggling cases before the Admiralty Courts—courts with appointed judges and no juries. The British government was unhappy that colonial juries often sympathized with smugglers and did not convict them in the colonial courts. But some colonists believed that taking away the right of trial by jury in these cases violated their rights as British citizens.

In 1765, Parliament passed the Stamp Act. Every official government document, as well as newspapers, almanacs, and even playing cards, needed to be

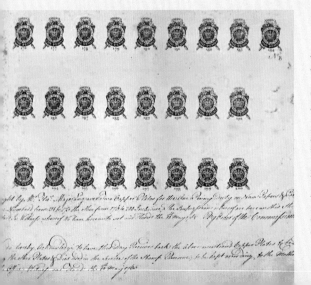

A sheet of tax stamps, which were required on all legal documents, permits, contracts, newspapers, pamphlets, and playing cards in the American colonies. The money raised from the Stamp Act tax was to be used to help pay the cost of protecting the colonies.

printed on paper *embossed* with an official stamp in advance of printing. A stamp tax had been collected in Great Britain since the late 1600s.

But the British Parliament had never before attempted to tax the colonies in this way. Each colony had its own legislature, which levied taxes to raise the money needed to run the colony. Many colonists strongly objected to the stamp tax. They reasoned that, because they were not permitted to vote in British parliamentary elections, Parliament did not have the right to tax them. "No taxation without representation!" became a popular slogan among these colonists.

Protests swept through the colonies. Organizations known as the *Sons of Liberty* formed up and down the Atlantic coast. Just five years after British and colonial soldiers had worked together to defeat the French, some radical members of the Sons of Liberty were even advocating armed resistance to British rule.

In October 1765, representatives from nine colonies gathered in New York for a meeting called the Stamp Act Congress. They agreed that Parliament did not have the power to tax the colonies and that Admiralty Courts did not have jurisdiction in the colonies. The congress also sent petitions to the king and Parliament demanding the repeal of the Sugar Act and the Stamp Act.

Amid cries of "Treason!" Patrick Henry presents resolutions against the Stamp Act to the Virginia House of Burgesses, May 30, 1765. The resolutions asserted that the colonists could not be taxed because they were not represented in Parliament.

Astonished by the colonial resistance, Parliament eventually repealed the Stamp Act. But this proved only a temporary victory for colonists who rejected Britain's right to tax them; Parliament would try again.

Just two years later, the Townshend Acts imposed new import taxes on a variety of goods, including lead, glass, paint, paper, and tea. Again, the colonists protested. The threat of violence grew, and in 1768, two British regiments arrived in Boston to help protect the customs officers. Colonists like Samuel Adams believed the arrival of troops showed that Parliament had no regard for the rights of the colonies. He and others urged resistance, but most colonists were not yet ready to defy the British government openly. From Massachusetts to Virginia, colonial organizations like the Sons of Liberty adopted non-importation agreements, by which they agreed not to import any item that was taxed under the Townshend Acts. Their hope was to inflict financial hardships on the British suppliers of the taxed goods. It worked.

By early 1770, Parliament had repealed all of the Townshend taxes except for the tax on tea. Although this represented a victory for the colonists, by keeping the tea tax Parliament was asserting its continued right to levy taxes on the colonies. The Sons of

fast fact...

The citizens of Great Britain had long paid many of the same taxes that the colonists protested. For example, they had paid a stamp tax for more than 70 years when the Stamp Act for the American colonies passed in 1765.

Liberty found this unacceptable and called for the boycott of British goods to continue until Parliament repealed the tax on tea as well. Popular support collapsed, however, and British goods once again flowed into the colonies.

Tea was widely popular in the colonies. The Tea Act of 1773 promised to make the beverage more affordable by allowing the British East India Company to sell tea directly to consumers in the American colonies, without having to pay certain import taxes. But the act also contained provisions that rubbed many colonists the wrong way. It gave the British East India Company a monopoly on selling tea in the colonies, angering colonial merchants who would be cut out of the tea trade. And the Townshend tax on tea remained in force.

The Sons of Liberty warned colonists that this was a scheme to get colonial acceptance of Parliament's right to tax them. As new shipments of tea arrived in colonial ports, protests prevented the tea from being unloaded. Many ships returned to Britain with their cargoes of tea still on board. In Boston, Thomas Hutchinson, the royal governor, refused to allow the ships to leave port until the tea was unloaded. An uneasy standoff ended in December 1773, when a *Patriot* mob boarded the vessels and tossed the cargo of tea into the harbor. The Boston Tea Party brought quick punishment from the British government.

On June 1, 1774, the British closed the port of Boston until the colonists paid for the destroyed tea. As a city dependent on trade, Boston suffered a heavy economic toll from this closure. But Parliament passed other new measures in 1774 that provoked the colonists' ire. One act changed the way the government of the colony of Massachusetts operated, replacing many elected positions with ones appointed by the king or royal governor. Another act allowed for government and customs officials accused of a crime in the colonies to face trial in Britain. Still another revised an

On the evening of December 16, 1773, a group of about 60 Patriots, some dressed as Mohawk Indians, boarded three ships in Boston Harbor and destroyed 342 crates of tea.

This drawing by Paul Revere shows Redcoats rowing into Boston from British warships anchored in the harbor. Britain's effort to punish Boston Patriots by closing the harbor generated sympathy for the Patriot cause throughout the colonies.

earlier bill so that colonial villages, towns, and cities were now required to lodge, when deemed necessary, British soldiers in inns, public houses, and even the barns, stables, and unoccupied buildings of private landowners rather than in separate military barracks. To emphasize their newfound authority under this last act, the British quartered troops in Boston.

The colonists dubbed these new bills "the Intolerable Acts." The Sons of Liberty convinced a growing number of colonists that Britain intended to enslave them. The Intolerable Acts, according to the Sons of Liberty, represented just one more step toward denying colonists their rights as British citizens.

To add fuel to the fire, Parliament passed the Quebec Act of 1774. Since the end of the French and Indian War, a military government had ruled Quebec, and this new act established a permanent government in the province without an elected legislature. It also recognized French civil law and granted protection to the Catholic Church in Quebec. While these measures were a source of concern among some colonists, another provision of the Quebec Act would stir up widespread anger. The act expanded the boundaries of Quebec to include all territory west of the Appalachian Mountains and north of the Ohio River. This was territory claimed by many colonies, including Pennsylvania and Virginia, in the heart of the Ohio River valley.

The combination of the Intolerable Acts, the harsh treatment of Boston following the Boston Tea Party, and the adoption of the Quebec Act rallied the colonists. By the fall of 1774, the colonies united to oppose what they considered British misrule.

The BLOODY MASSACRE perpetrated in King——Street Boston on March 5th 1770 by

Engrav'd Printed & Sold by PAUL REVERE

Unhappy BOSTON! see thy Sons deplore,
Thy hallow'd Walks besmear'd with guiltless Gore:
While faithless P——n and his savage Bands,
With murd'rous Rancour stretch their bloody Hands;
Like fierce Barbarians grinning o'er their Prey,
Approve the Carnage, and enjoy the Day.

If scalding drops from Rage from Anguish Wrung,
If speechless Sorrows lab'ring for a Tongue,
Or if a weeping World can ought appease
The plaintive Ghosts of Victims such as these;
The Patriot's copious Tears for each are shed,
A glorious Tribute which embalms the Dead

But know, Fate
Where JUSTICE
Should venal
Snatch the re
Keen Execra
Shall reach a

The unhappy Sufferers were Mess.rs SAM.L GRAY, SAM.L MAVERICK, JAM.S CALDWELL, CR
Killed. Six wounded; two of them (CHRIST.R MONK & JOHN CLARK) Mo
Published in 1770 by P

Paul Revere's engraving of a March 1770 clash between Patriots and Redcoats became the most famous picture of the Boston Massacre. In Revere's version, the British troops open fire on defenseless civilians—excellent propaganda, but not quite the way it happened.

5

Growing Tensions

In September 1774, delegates from 12 of the American colonies attended the First Continental Congress in Philadelphia, Pennsylvania. Georgia was the only colony that did not send representatives. The *committees of correspondence* throughout the colonies had urged that a congress meet to discuss options to oppose the growing British threat to colonial freedoms.

Those calling for open rebellion were still in the minority, but the Continental Congress did approve an agreement called "the Association," by which the 12 colonies promised not to import or consume any goods from Great Britain, Ireland, or the British West Indies. They also agreed not to export any goods to these countries. The Continental Congress also sent to Parliament a proposal that most colonial affairs be left to the colonial legislatures, and it appealed to Parliament to revoke the Intolerable Acts. Before adjourning, the Continental Congress agreed to meet again in May 1775.

At this point, a full-fledged war between Great Britain and the American colonies was not inevitable. Still, incidents of violence that had taken place over the past decade had hardened the views of some people on both sides. During the Stamp Act crisis of 1765, violent opposition to the act erupted in Boston and New York. In Boston, a mob broke into the home of the local stamp distributor. In New York, the British governor had to take the stamped paper to Fort George under guard. A mob of nearly 2,000 threatened to storm the fort and destroy the stamps, but instead they burned the home of a British officer who had promised to force the New Yorkers to accept the stamp tax.

In the late 1760s and early 1770s, colonial mobs frequently targeted the Crown's tax and customs collectors. Many of these officials were intimidated into resigning, while others suffered physical assaults. As a result, the British government found it difficult to fill these posts in many areas.

The growing number of British soldiers stationed in cities such as New York and Boston raised tensions with the colonists. In New York in January 1770, the "battle of Golden Hill" erupted after British soldiers repeatedly cut down the liberty pole erected by the Sons of Liberty in a public green. While there were many wounded colonists and soldiers, no one died this time. That would change two months later.

On March 5, 1770, a mob gathered outside Boston's Customs House and pelted the British soldiers guarding the building with snow, ice, sticks, and rocks. Finally, the soldiers opened fire, killing five and wounding six others. Though the colonists had provoked the confrontation, Sons of Liberty members like Samuel Adams and Paul Revere were able to use the incident to portray the British as killers. Revere's inflammatory engraving of the Boston Massacre circulated widely throughout the colonies.

As tensions between the colonies and Great Britain grew, so too did divisions within the colonies. Opinions among the colonists varied greatly. While some leaders, such as Isaac Sears in New York and Samuel Adams in Boston, called for armed conflict and independence, others continued to support the king's government and Parliament's authority. Most colonists were somewhere in the middle. Between the Stamp

Benjamin Franklin stands before the British Privy Council on January 29, 1774. As the official representative of the American colonies, Franklin had tried to peacefully resolve the growing disagreements between British and colonial leaders. However, at this government hearing Franklin was

Act of 1765 and the Quebec Act of 1774, more and more colonists found themselves taking sides. Those supporting the king and the British government were called *Loyalists.* Patriots (or Rebels) were those who defied British law and supported colonial rights. As more colonists developed strong feelings one way or the other, the chances for reconciliation grew dimmer.

When the petitions from the First Continental Congress finally arrived in London, Parliament

unfairly accused of instigating the Boston Tea Party and other Patriot activities. This incident helped Franklin realize that the Americans would never have the same rights as other British citizens. He soon returned to the colonies and began working actively for American independence.

declined to respond to any of the requests. War between Great Britain and its North American colonies now appeared likely. King George III was among those who regarded a conflict as inevitable. In late 1774, the English monarch had stated, "The New England Governments are in a State of Rebellion. Blows must decide whether they are to be subject to this Country or Independent."

The Patriots who fought for independence during the American Revolution persevered despite many hardships. The determination of Continental Army soldiers is captured in Archibald M. Willard's famous painting *Spirit of '76.*

6

The American War of Independence

T he outbreak of fighting at Lexington and Concord, Massachusetts, on April 19, 1775, marked the official beginning of the American War of Independence. Yet in a certain sense, the American Revolution had started much earlier, when the American colonists resisted the Sugar Act and the Stamp Act. "The Revolution," as John Adams observed, "was in the minds and hearts of the people" before the first shots were fired in anger.

Yet even after the bloodshed at Lexington and Concord, some colonists continued to hope for a peaceful reconciliation with the British government. As events unfolded in the spring of 1775, however, that hope quickly receded. Three weeks after Lexington and

Concord, Ethan Allen and Benedict Arnold led an army of Patriots that captured Fort Ticonderoga without firing a shot. On the same day, May 10, 1775, the Second Continental Congress convened in Philadelphia. Following the Battle of Bunker Hill outside Boston in June 1775, it became evident to both the British and the Continentals that this was a real war.

When the Continental Congress adopted the Declaration of Independence on July 4, 1776, it created a new nation, the United States of America. For five more years, the Continental Army, led by General George Washington, fought to earn American independence. It was a difficult struggle with many setbacks. Great Britain fielded the best-trained and best-equipped army in the world. British troops occupied Boston, Charleston, and Philadelphia at some point during the war, and the British held on to New York City from 1776 to 1783.

Colonists fought on both sides, and all faced hardships. Living conditions in military camps were difficult. Armies often lacked sufficient food to feed the troops. Diseases ran rampant: for every soldier killed in the fighting, disease claimed the lives of 10 others. Civilians also suffered. Patriots and Loyalists alike risked losing their homes. As armies moved through an area, they scavenged for food and firewood, often

Members of the committee assigned to draft the Declaration of Independence—John Adams, Roger Sherman, Robert Livingston, Thomas Jefferson, and Benjamin Franklin—present the document to John Hancock, president of the Second Continental Congress, in June 1776.

tearing down houses to feed the cooking fires.

An American victory at Yorktown, Virginia, in October 1781 marked the end of major fighting, but it was two more years before the Treaty of Paris formally ended the war and Great Britain officially recognized the independence of the United States. The British had lost their American colonies.

Great Britain and the colonies had steadily drifted apart after the French and Indian War. Even before that conflict, the colonial legislatures had grown accustomed to conducting the daily affairs of the

The British surrender at Yorktown, Virginia, in October 1781 marked the end of major combat in the American Revolution. The war officially ended when British and American officials signed a peace treaty in Paris on September 3, 1783.

colonies with little interference from the British Parliament. Many colonists resisted Parliament's attempts to tax them in order to help pay for the costs of the French and Indian War. By 1775, the rift between the colonies and the mother country had grown too bitter to mend.

It is possible, had cooler heads prevailed both in Parliament and in the colonies, that the American Revolution could have been avoided. Eventually, however, it is likely that Britain and the colonies would have parted ways. Maybe the war would have happened later in history, or maybe Britain would have granted the United States independence in the way Canada received its independence in 1867—with the passing of a law.

But the American Revolution did happen, and its impact extended well beyond the shores of North America. The Marquis de Lafayette had fought for American independence before returning to France to become a leader in the French Revolution of 1789. Mexico threw off Spanish rule in 1810, and the nations of South America soon followed. Many of the leaders in these wars of independence looked to the United States for inspiration. Similarly, nations in Europe and beyond emulated the *republican* form of government embraced by the United States as they developed new governments throughout the 19th and even 20th centuries. The American Revolution was truly a turning point in the history of the world.

Chronology

1607   The English colony at Jamestown, Virginia, is established.

1620   The Pilgrims arrive at Plymouth, Massachusetts.

1754   George Washington is defeated at Fort Necessity, in western Pennsylvania, as the French and Indian War begins. Delegates from nine British colonies meet with Iroquois leaders at the Albany Congress, where Benjamin Franklin's proposal for a union of the colonies for mutual defense is adopted (but it is never enacted by the individual colonial assemblies).

1760   The surrender of Montreal by the French marks the end of the French and Indian War in North America.

1763   The Seven Years' War ends in Europe. Deep in debt, Great Britain passes the Sugar Act, with enforcement measures to collect taxes on sugar and molasses in the American colonies.

1765   The passage of the Stamp Act causes widespread protest in the colonies. The Stamp Act Congress meets in October to protest the tax, stating that it exceeds Parliament's authority over the colonies.

1766   Parliament repeals the Stamp Act.

1767   The Townshend duties on lead, paper, glass, paint, and tea are passed by Parliament. The colonies adopt non-importation agreements, promising not to buy goods from Great Britain until the Townshend duties are repealed.

1768   Two British regiments arrive in Boston to help enforce customs and tax laws.

1770   British troops at the Customs House in Boston open fire on a protesting mob, killing five colonists. The colonists call this the Boston Massacre.

1773   The Tea Act gives the British East India Company a monopoly on the sale of tea in the colonies. Colonists in Boston dump a shipment of tea into the harbor.

1774   Great Britain closes the port of Boston as part of "the Intolerable Acts." The Quebec Act expands the borders of Quebec to include the land north of the Ohio River. The First Continental Congress meets in Philadelphia in September.

1775   The battles at Lexington and Concord in April begin the American Revolution.

1776   The United States of America declares its independence on July 4.

1781   The British defeat at the Battle of Yorktown in October marks the end of major fighting during the American Revolution.

1783   The Treaty of Paris formally ends the American Revolution. Great Britain recognizes American independence.

Glossary

cash crop—a crop grown primarily because it can easily be sold at market.

colonization—the process by which a country makes claim to and settles land outside its borders.

committee of correspondence—a pre–Revolutionary War organization that was maintained by a colonial assembly and whose purpose was to share legislative and political developments with the assemblies of other colonies.

confiscate—to seize the property of an individual or group (typically by government authority).

craze—a fad or extremely popular activity or practice.

defensive works—fortifications, often made of wood, earth, or stone, built to protect troops from an attack.

embossed—having a raised design created by the stamping of paper or another flat surface.

grievances—a list of complaints or concerns.

Loyalists—those who remained loyal to King George III and the British government during the American Revolution.

magazine—a room where gunpowder and explosives are stored.

militia—nonprofessional troops called upon during an emergency to fight the enemy. When not needed, militia troops remain at home and go about their daily lives.

minutemen—the militia of Massachusetts, who were supposed to drop everything at a minute's notice and pick up arms to defend their towns.

Nonconformists—members of any of a number of religious groups in England and the American colonies who did not accept all the teachings of the Anglican Church (also known as the Church of England).

Parliament—the elected legislature of Great Britain, from which the king or queen chose the prime minister and other ministers.

Patriot—a colonist who opposed Parliament and King George III before and during the American Revolution.

petition—a formal written request made to a government leader or official body.

proclamation—a declaration by the government setting new policies or new rules.

provincial—a person from one of the British colonies in North America; relating to the British North American colonies.

republican—relating to or characteristic of a government in which leaders are elected by popular vote and represent the interests of the people.

Sons of Liberty—a group of Patriots organized to resist British attempts to take away colonial rights in the years leading up to the American Revolution.

tidewater—low coastal lands that drain into the tidal waters.

Further Reading

Books for Students:

Herbert, Janis. *The American Revolution for Kids: A History with 21 Activities.* Chicago: Chicago Review Press, 2002.

Marrin, Albert. *George Washington and the Founding of a Nation.* New York: Dutton, 2001.

Moore, Kay. *If You Lived at the Time of the American Revolution.* Illustrated by Daniel O'Leary. New York: Scholastic, 1998.

Murphy, Jim. *A Young Patriot: The American Revolution as Experienced by One Boy.* New York: Clarion Books, 1998.

Murray, Stuart. *Eyewitness: American Revolution.* New York: Dorling Kindersley Publishing, 2002.

Books for Older Readers:

Ellis, Joseph J. *Founding Brothers: The Revolutionary Generation.* New York: Vintage, 2002.

Fleming, Thomas. *Liberty! The American Revolution.* New York: Viking, 1997.

Isaacson, Walter. *Benjamin Franklin: An American Life.* New York: Simon & Schuster, 2003.

Middlekauff, Robert. *The Glorious Cause: The American Revolution, 1763–1789.* 2nd edition. New York: Oxford University Press, 2005.

Wood, Gordon S. *The American Revolution: A History.* New York: Modern Library, 2002.

http://www.nps.gov/revwar

This National Park Service website includes links to numerous American Revolutionary War sites. It also features a time line, biographies, and educational resources related to America's War of Independence.

http://www.pbs.org/ktca/liberty/

This site evolved from the PBS program on the American Revolution, *Liberty!*

http://americanrevwar.homestead.com

Biographies, time lines, and descriptions of the events that led up to the American Revolution, as well as the war itself.

http://www.americaslibrary.gov/cgi-bin/page.cgi/jb/
    revolut

This site from the Library of Congress offers information about different events and people from the American Revolution.

http://www.bbc.co.uk/history/british/empire_seapower/
    american_revolution_01.shtml

This website produced by the British Broadcasting Corporation (BBC) asks and answers the question "Was the American Revolution inevitable?"

Index

Numbers in **bold italics** refer to captions.

Picture Credits

About the Author

RICHARD M. STRUM was born in Ticonderoga, New York. He earned his BA at Houghton College and MAEd at the College of William and Mary. Rich is the Director of Interpretation & Education at Fort Ticonderoga. He is also the author of *Ticonderoga: Lake Champlain Steamboat*, a book for adults about the last passenger steamboat on Lake Champlain, and *Fort Ticonderoga*, a book for children. He lives in Ferrisburgh, Vermont, with his wife Martha and daughters Mackenzie and Kirsten.